What It Must Be Like for You

Other works by Dennis Sampson

The Double Genesis

Forgiveness

Constant Longing

Needlegrass

For my Father Falling Asleep at Saint Mary's Hospital

Within the Shadow of a Man

The Lunatic in the Trees

Selected Poems

What More Could the Universe Want

What It Must Be Like for You

Dennis Sampson

Homestead Lighthouse Press
Grants Pass, Oregon

Copyright © Dennis Sampson, 2024. All rights reserved. No part of this book may be reproduced or transmitted in any form without the prior written permission of the publisher.

Library of Congress Cataloging-in-Publication Data
    Names: Sampson, Dennis, 1949-author.
    Title: *What It Must Be Like for You* / Dennis Sampson.
    Description: Homestead Lighthouse Press. Grants Pass, OR Homestead Lighthouse Press, 2019

ISBN 978-1-950475-37-7
Library of Congress Control Number: 2024934856

    Homestead Lighthouse Press
    1668 NE Foothill Boulevard
    Unit A
    Grants Pass, OR 97526
www.homesteadlighthousepress.com

Distributed by Homestead Lighthouse Press, Amazon.com, Barnes & Noble

Homestead Lighthouse Press gratefully acknowledges the generous support of its readers and patrons.

Book cover and interior design by Ray Rhamey, Ashland, OR

For Ed

Table Of Contents

This Late Autumn's Spell — 1
It was an isolated place of meditation — 2
Late Life — 3
Finding Your Way In This World — 5
Aurora Borealis — 7

One

All — 10
Firstborn — 12
In Pursuit Of The Expressionless Gazelle — 13
The Roach — 14
Small Potatoes — 15
The Mystery; A Prayer For Me — 17
Blue cottonwoods new in the wind — 19

Two

Still Alive On Shattalon Drive — 21
Show me your tits — 23
The chip shot dribbled — 25
Looking Across The Field Watching The Birds Fly — 26
What could be more humbling for an intelligent tree — 27
Sunrise showing up again in my summer window — 28
My inattentiveness to this wandering world — 29
I thought of going straight home from the liquor store — 31

Three

It cost me my childhood in order to see	34
Sun and Moon	35
What's this that I see	36
A Dog, My God, My Dog a God	38
The elegiac feeling comes and goes	39
One For The Rose From Fresno	41
I don't know about you	42
The Swan's Song	43
You were so close	44

Four

You should never use the word beautiful	48
Blue Estuaries	49
I would like to be kinder	50
Silent	52
I let the handyman in	53
This Ancient Study	54
I've come to love the freckled middle-aged face of Lori	55
And there where the garden path on November mornings	57

Five

That Disconcerting Epiphany	59
I had to laugh	61
Who wouldn't want to understand	62
Neither Tony nor Jane nor Lucia can see	63
In The Cool Heart Of Morning	65
This is my life, not yours	67

Six

Galilee	69
Last Leaf	70
Should I have lingered longer	71
Night in the fields. And the new moon there.	72
What More Might There Be For You To Say?	73
Let that moth fighting for her life	74
Old Age	76
He had hoped	78
What must it be like for you, you	80
John Clare	81
For Over Fifty Years	83
Can I Give You This	84

Gone, the sweet agitation of the breath of Pan.

Robert Lowell

This Late Autumn's Spell

Speaking ceases and the spell is cast.
Even the rude blue jay's strident cry is nowhere to be heard

on the porch that I occupy that seems all the world.
Such silence.

It is the spiritual interim,
the silence that encourages the soul to take it all in.

No birds
No wind.

It was an isolated place of meditation

fleshed out by planes of light,
a quivering sanctuary of silver and gold filaments
for the mind that had withdrawn,
the mind that had come forth.
Light pouring at an angle through the forest.

What darker purposes there were
were not important:
hidden, alert - the daughter of dark beauty. The wet
strands trembled and shined. And yet if I stood
adjacent to this remote and solitary home
it passed from sight, as if it too had a mind of its own.

One who just by chance had stopped to marvel
at this fascinator's craft
leans back, a symmetry conceived of from within
while that spider knits fastidiously inward until at last
there's this - both for the mind
withdrawn, and for the mind that had come forth.

Late Life

That's me, being intimate.
All that baloney about the meaning of life.

Well, it wasn't baloney some 20 years ago.
I was earnest.

But I couldn't find the tone so anyone would listen to my wonderment,
running my fingertips up and down the forearm of a woman
that I loved.

Start here and go in any direction.
It's a lot like the notion that if you're falling through space,

with no lights around you then falling isn't really falling.
You always stay where you are.

The Eskimo in a blizzard staring for days at a snowman in the Arctic
so he won't go out of his mind.

Start with the yellow daffodil.
A petal. A stamen.

For that matter, begin working your way in
from way out in the cosmos.

Microcosm,
Macrocosm.

One way or another,
you're going to find out it was all
in the trying to understand why.

Finding Your Way In This World

He was a person. He put
one foot in front of the other and frequently

thought of himself before thinking of others,
fought for words to ask a woman whom he loved

what he had done wrong and sobbed
during a counseling session in a back room of

a Catholic church when his wife made it clear she
did not want him to touch her. He smoked,

wrote in enclosures that were cold, that were sweltering,
and celebrated his modest accomplishments

by drinking alone in a small bar in Cleveland Heights,
infuriating those who did not like his kind

of frankness. When his mother gave up her ghost
not long after her stroke, he felt lost. The singularly

vivid iridescent streak of sunlight in late afternoon
inspired him to write, as did that one star stationed brazenly

beside the quarter moon one night while he
was thinking of what Mars was like. He never forgot

the aroma of Mennen after-shave permeating
the hallway
when his father left the bathroom hiking up his pants,

the sweet fragrance of purple lilacs blossoming in all corners
of the yard. A person –
soul among souls. Three posh nights on a honeymoon

in Captiva, room service, Pina Coladas, a day
in the Floridian sun. He could not get enough of lionesses,

their charcoal noses soaked with wildebeest blood,
lounging on their backs in the shade of an acacia tree in Kenya,

yawning. And he once cupped a leopard frog after a splash
and was startled by how desperately it wanted to get out.

Aurora Borealis

What a beautiful name.
I saw it in awe for the first time with my father
who had his hands in his hip pockets

at night in our front yard, along Riverview Avenue.

It rippled and enlarged.

And I wonder if what went through my father's mind
was the same as what went through mine.

Will you weep with me for just a moment or so
regarding the passage of time?

Jesus wept
at the sight of the human city.

Just as Ruth did amid the alien corn. The surprise of death
as a child turned me further and further inward

and it took me what seemed like decades to see
the Little Dipper as it was described by my father.

Beautiful child,
almost as if I, now, were the father of that child looking up

once again, circa 1959. And I seem to realize
that this captivated and captivating little cleric

is imagining me writing this down, lines left to right
with my dog's chin lain across the lower part of my arm.

One

All

Nothing more: season
after season. And within
each day, day darkened.
By thunderstorms. By rain
that rained on Plotinus
holding up his garment.

God was there, then
was not, what it is like
to be defined and redefined,
the sugar maple weighted with
late autumn's first fall
of snow, all, all. In the event
you should come across

the excrement of a fawn
through which a trillium
opens wildly, you'll know.
Otherwise you'll go on
searching for all in Eve's
and Adam's fall, such

loveliness of breasts, thighs,
lips, toes: the black spot
on the wall a moth, spooked
by your hand's shadow,
that unpalatable apple: the serpent
with sleazy fingers to meet alluring

Eve half way. Eve reaching,
then snow, then thaw,
drought, thirst. Menstruation,
conception. That first child.

Firstborn

Nothing to fear. Your frightened father carries you
cradled in his arms in the half dark.
He is reciting Lear

knowing one daughter out of three will despair.
But you are not that daughter, Una.

Stars in the west window ajar in a quiet house
one month after your birth
shine down.
They are shining on you, Una,
you who must surely wonder intuitively
what a father is doing uttering Shakespeare,

that nothing will come of nothing, spoken so softly
as if by a ghost
beyond the two of you there.

Una turning golden in the morning,
this first summer of yours
drifting with your frightened father from light to shadow

shadow to the light before the latticed window.
You can sleep now.
You and your father are the truth.

In Pursuit Of The Expressionless Gazelle

The story? It begins with death. Before that death though
there's bafflement on your father's face when he realizes
you can actually play the trombone fairly well, there is
that side-long glimpse of your mother in middle age smoking
with an ashtray in her lap menthol cigarettes on the couch,
and the dream of doing something spectacular like rescuing
Kathy Gallimore in fifth grade from being hit by a truck. This story
begins and ends with what both was and is, a honey bee hustling
around a marigold that gave you the kind of hesitation as a kid
that would influence the way you live. Or maybe the afternoon
you took the elevator at Saint Mary's hospital to the fourth floor
above where your father was rotting away with prostate cancer
to commiserate with an old friend
who had given up everything to be there for her demented sister

and immediately inhaled the overwhelming stench of shit, the sister,
daft, who slipped away from her bed and fluttered gaily up and down
the polished hallway with no mind of her own, staring no less
than an inch from your face, wild-eyed, as if you weren't there. The
logic spins like this: if you are compassionate then death
is for those who have had their back broken by brute force
cinched with twine, to make the corpse easier to carry, and this
begins and ends for everyone of us as it did for the exhausted
Grant's gazelle hunted down by wild dogs in the glow and heat
of the Masai Maura, death preferable to taking one more step.

The Roach

It panics in the porcelain sink
like Simon Peter after his final lie

when I switch on the light beside the refrigerator
then skates unsuccessfully up against those insurmountable walls

before it finds sanctuary again in the vortex
from which this roach decided to make an appearance

in search of what I left behind in my haste.
I live alone. And therefore pause

over such trivial absurdities.

The mouse that always seems to be the first mouse
on its haunches,
tiny eyes lifted sweetly to me from its elysium of sunflower seeds.

One old roach.
One mouse.

No doubt you may take issue with my eccentric behavior here
or simply do not give a damn. It is this
that makes me second guess myself before doing anything
to either of them.

What the hell. And why not?
Let each and every one of them live forever.

Small Potatoes

Childish, I suppose,
entertaining a little frivolously in one of my reveries
that Jesus must have had hiccups
at least once after a swallow of wine passed on to him

at a long table. I see Jesus with his back to the fire in his filthy tunic,
his disciples on either side
all holding up their palms to the flames that bend and flare

with the fickle winds of Galilee,
devotees side by side making precisely the same gesture.

Oh, great silent one with the jerking up and down
of your shoulders every few seconds
wouldn't you, too, take a huge breath in the dark and hold it in?
Childish, I suppose.

Small potatoes compared to the heart attack Larry would have,
up nights trying to write the biography
of an unknown professional baseball player who ended up
killing himself after the third attempt that year.
Tearing the filters from his menthol cigarettes.

The history of humankind. It begins. It ends: with a hiccup.
A burp, the sneeze, the whistle, the slap on the back.
Kaboom, goes the universe. Ho-hum.

It's that myopic leopard frog as a study in stillness
whose plop in a now undulating pond
in seventeenth century China that opens the eyes of one man.

The Mystery; A Prayer For Me

Is what I have written down
for half a century a prayer?
And if so, what exactly is a prayer?
There are so many depictions of prayer for me.

Maybe everything you say when you are saying in so many words
"Let this cup pass from me" is a prayer.

My sister's whispered supplications in ICU that her comatose son sweet Nathan,
be given back to her after his overdose from heroin.
Was that a prayer?
Karen squeezed his flaccid hand while at the same time

gripping the stiffening fingers of her sister Linda.
It was not to be.

I pled after my divorce from Colleen.
But what I was pleading for remains an enigma to me.

Someone once and for all should tell me what prayer is.
My last old sensational dog in the back seat howling
because he had a slipped disc, was that a prayer?
Is asking for absolutely nothing

with your eyes closed and opening them into a deity
made small for man a prayer?
Is the magic number thirteen foreboding? Is the black
Siamese cat stepping with trepidation under a ladder an omen?

What is it all about, then?
Let us all go down on our knees
then reach upward in prayer.
Whatever prayer might be.

Blue cottonwoods new in the wind

and yellow grasses rising away on the horizon.
And the horizon as she has always been in wandering summer
drawn to autumn that is wandering too.

And all of the pain of winter on the reservation
where silhouettes no longer walk.

And the visible spirits that sang in unison
no longer the incantation
that was crimson and blue eucharist for me.

If I go there, what I see I see again.
Unfathomable past.
Everything one surely thought was true.

Blue trees in the evening western wind.
The wonder of why and wonder of what is loved.
The Missouri River of death, now the river of living.

And I am not here.
And I am here forever.

Two

Still Alive On Shattalon Drive

It's not often that I look up at my house from way
out in the yard. When I do, my imagination goes wild.

Who lives there?

What does who lives there do?

It is an almost apocalyptic alteration in perspective
the one living inside is deprived of,

a figure in profile,
sometimes in summer the front door cracked open to let out the dog.

Bill Evans on the piano playing *My Foolish Heart*
leaning over the keys like a jeweler examining a diamond.

This is where I live.
This is the old house.

Bestowed on the lover by the wealthy loved. Rent paid
promptly each month.
What does a man do with a woman
as practical as that?

Jane liked, in particular, the wide window upstairs
that allowed her to escape the blank page when she was trying

to write about being in exile.

I turn my chair around, late November,
cold after an intermittent drizzle that brimmed the dishes

for the gray squirrels

who after all these years still make it a point to see
if I am getting too close. And if so flee as if they were on fire.

Although I am there. And am here as never before. There. Elsewhere.

The pacing back-and-forth.
The lying down.
The getting up at night.

Show me your tits

the man cupping his hands under his breasts
shouted, jiggling them
alongside the wrought-iron railing
where Larry and I had a downward view
of the indolent gorillas that afternoon
at the Washington Zoo.

He was screaming
and looking up stupidly for our reaction
at one of the female apes
squatting underneath us with sagging dugs,
forlornly staring and holding
out her palm
to my friend of forty years eating an orange,
each strip of skin
tucked neatly in his pocket.
"Show me your tits!"

And I forgot however briefly in my reverie
what was the center of attention
until that gorilla
draped over mold-gray breasts
her long slender other arm after staring mournfully.
And there was sorrow
that had as its source
a sickening misunderstanding between one
consciousness and another,

the other gorillas eating bananas, watermelons,
Buddhas
with their massive backs turned away from tee shirts,
snow cones, cotton candy, binoculars.
A sorrow that still bothers me
walking and talking, waking and wondering
every waking minute of my life.

The chip shot dribbled

an analytical Titleist ball to the rim of the cup
while I was wincing
underneath the sprinkler that went around

and around and around. Still, I could see my father's hand
sparkle in the sun
above where he genuflected on the 18th green in the sand trap

then pathetically smiled when, faking dismay,
he saw what a lucky son of a bitch he was making par.

Riding home my father did let me have a long drink
from the can of cold Storz beer.
My God.
That taste was wondrous.

I love my father.
But how do you look at someone who has lied

the way you looked at him before
you saw that little white hand flip up
a golf ball
on the 18th green then step aside from the sprinkler

with a half-witted grin as if you even at the age of 13
were as dumb as a doorknob?

Looking Across The Field Watching The Birds Fly

I think it was Vaughn who said "I saw eternity
the other night." That first line: I thought it was simultaneously

preposterous and inspiring.

And my robust authoritative fellow poet Robert
alone
in Dickinson's bedroom, one of the hushed tourists,
convinced that at some point that hovering phantom

in her white wrap settled her fragile hand
on his shoulder while he was sitting politely at her desk in the dark.

But don't you know that those droplets on that clay vase
on the painting by Velazquez had me in awe?

Eternity – a
tireless inquisitor.
A moth wandering about.

Wasn't it Pascal who had that horrifying vision of a soul
and scribbled the word *Fire!*
on a piece of parchment and sewed it into his breast pocket?

Wasn't it Cezanne who left a little
of the apple in a still-life unfinished
because he couldn't quite figure it out?

What could be more humbling for an intelligent tree

I have seen for the first time
than to have to capitulate to this drizzle turned to sleet?

It is not pleased. So I pull down
the lowest hanging branch of that genius that has no name

and let crystals shower down on me.
After that, this anonymous beauty seems to regain

what it always wanted to be. Those familial branches spring
upward. One more shake. Then shudder. Then release.

Sunrise showing up again in my summer window

daughter of my ancient heart, you are here
shyly climbing ever so deliberately through the Magnolia
in my dark backyard.
And your presence entices the faintest of first songs.

I'd get up too and watch what you will do to the only world I know.
But I'm still so tired.
You're going to have to wait Ra
another day or so for my irrelevant attention

while opening your endless arms to me.
The rising of the sun,
the sun that belongs to us on this accommodating planet,
innocently spinning through the oblivion

of beginning and middle and end and what
might come after that
just as it belongs to itself
and to no one.

My inattentiveness to this wandering world

of mine shows itself
when I am stretching with my arms way up in the air
on the porch with my Chow

that nudges his cold black nose into my opening palm
when I let it down. That rooster,
the one I had listened to for years.
It was responding to another equally adamant,

three lots down.

They were sure of themselves. Confident. So full of bravado.
And they wanted each other to know that.
One egotistical pronouncement of pure joy up close

with the almost inaudible potentate answering in kind.
How could I have missed that discourse for so long?

 Oh let them go at it until the end of time.
Two little crowing titans both at dawn and at dusk.

The mind knows the importance of such back and forths,
the mind that is of the one
silent on the newly painted porch in his blue and white bathrobe

although it was well below freezing in Winston-Salem.
And I can't help but visualize
those courtesans clucking and strutting underneath him,

so proud of one so proud. Mussolini.
John the Baptist. Caligula. Franco with his impudent nose
lifted and sniffing as if he had caught the scent.

I thought of going straight home from the liquor store

this beautiful morning and on a whim turned off
to where I knew there was water,
a faraway pond that changes from viridescent to brown

each season and that I've circled too many times to count
not because I can't stomach what I see of the world,
but because looking long at a body of water, my car on the shoulder

off Balsom road, is as reassuring as the palm of a mother's vast hand
open across your forehead when you had the mumps

and were on your back in your pajamas on a school day
in the double bed that she slept in so often face to face with your father.

It doesn't hurt to have a gaggle of geese in defiance
waddling before you there.

What could be more poignant than seeing six goslings
put their trust in their upright Mother Superior?

Ah, wide water
like the river where Louie and I set up our lawn chairs

outside Eutaw, Alabama that I had bought at Walmart the day before
with this precise idea in mind, pulling one frosty Budweiser

then another from the styrofoam cooler after a hit of pot
and cracking them open with the loveliest of scents

watching, not saying a word, a single stork
move smoothly upriver that both of us looked at in awe.

Three

It cost me my childhood in order to see

who I was without being frightened. I have
to give special credit to that disgusted-with-my awful life
flop-eared clown trying to light a cigarette off to the side of me

for another clown, a purple petunia sprouting
from his cranium painted white, cupping his alabaster hands

beside the bleachers at a rodeo in Fort Pierre in 1959. The Brahma
bull
bucked against the injustice
of it all. And I was in the process of transitioning

 from being naive to being miserable with knowledge
by what had just seemed like a frolicking nincompoop to me.

It is like Heisenberg's Principle of Uncertainty. You see it
then you don't. Look away then look back.

And you are not only that otherworldly child, eyes straying

away from other eyes, your still young father's eyes among them,
a cowboy flipped up
from the backbone of a Brahma bull that is pissed,

but the one who sees that after a lifetime
to put pressure on yourself to get it right is wrong.

Sun and Moon
(for Jane Mead)

What a wonder. And such sorrow too.
You look away from what you're doing

and you see not only the sun
but the moon.

It is a marriage of two solitudes. The attraction
one feels for the other is so clear.

I always hoped Jane would learn to look up with me.
She always had her head down

shuffling toward me across the brick patio on her way
to the English department at Wake Forest, with a book

of contemporary poetry pressed against her chest. She just
couldn't do it. To turn inward.

Immeasurable depths. Who is pursuing who across
the sky this evening?
Such wonder. And such sorrow too.

What's this that I see

I say to myself,
my whole head out the window of my old Corolla

slowed to a crawl, but those dark gray rolling clouds
in El Greco's *Toledo in a Thunderstorm*?

And who are they in flip flops and on bare feet seen
from such a long way off before endlessly incoming waves
from my cramped balcony,

but those of a watercolor with stupendous mountains capped
in white in the background, in ancient Szechuan, China.

When my black cat named Joe Louis stopped melodramatically
in front of the only plant
in my apartment just prior to my divorce from Colleen

my sympathetic friend and I saw what we remembered immediately –
those flagrant childlike paintings by that most forgotten of artists

Henri Rousseau. Those personas that have followed me
through my surprisingly long life. That's Klimpt

I think to myself, taking my foot off the pedal
before a stand
of birches in winter on my drive outside Winston-Salem,
for to do otherwise would

mean that I have not learned a thing
about what it means to be
a writer in our time. That's the sunlight on the side
of a house that Hopper wanted to get down.

A Dog, My God, My Dog A God

in the middle of this night
drinking water: the pendants on his collar
click the sides of his dish. I don't need another sound
right now. This one's fine with me. Then I remember
the mule's hooves in the French Quarter when I walked
the wet streets with Liz. The clop clop clop
comes back, after three decades.
Have you ever listened to an infant
asleep in a cradle singing?
Suzanne's daughter use to do that
and I'd conceal myself beside her door.
It was like overhearing a rumor whispered between
one angel and another. My dog
thirsts. He draws the lukewarm water in, pauses,
a perfectly ordinary sound, like ice
when the cocktail glass is lifted to the lips,
provisional and hurrying footsteps
you follow outside a window and know who it is.
What Emily Dickinson evidently did
listening like a prisoner
from her candlelit second floor in Amherst.

The elegiac feeling comes and goes

for me. The sorrow of the falling snow here in habitual December
seems now absurd. There is no sorrow in falling snow.

But there certainly is what I would call
going forward into the limited years

and the incendiary pleasure
when, as a child, my eyes opened slowly

to the snowdrift almost up
to our spacious living room window, flicked by wind.

This is not resignation, it is not precisely surrender.
Something *close* to saying the hell with it though.

As it was for the sculptor of the Burghers of Calais,
one two three four five six dignitaries in ashen gowns

summoned forward as fodder for he who had been triumphant.

One looked over his shoulder like Lot's disobedient wife
to those who could be no help to them anymore.

Even the elegiac feeling falls away after seven decades.
Why should I be any different than those who writhed
in incalculable numbers in Poland?

Herod giving it up along with Christ,
Linda Oldaker. Bobby Ellwanger
who played third base with me in 1968
in the last stage of his prostate cancer in Rapid City

finding reassurance in a passage from the Gospels.
Hitler goose-stepping through the universe.
Empedocles with Dante. Dante refusing.
Giotto painting like a child.

One For The Rose From Fresno

A cemetery in winter
is where I go, the gravestones as horrible
outside Miller, South Dakota
as any idea founded on the disposition to live

one hour more. I go there to remember who
I was. Just as a man goes back after twenty-four years
to Detroit to recover what escaped him
all of his life. And it was a life.

The foundries have woken up. Black smoke.
And the cemetery slides through the dawn
like a kid on a skateboard, eyes wide
while keeping his eye on the beautiful prize.

It was love. It was the breath of life
blown across your mouth when you
were a boy, older brother, in love, in love
with the baked potato that looks so much like us.

I don't know about you

but in the end
along with what I would consider unnecessary suffering,

there is such befuddlement that the kid who caught the high fly ball
to right field on the run through a blur of mosquitoes under the stadium lights

would look up with the old eyes he never thought he had
at a night nurse tapping an IV with her forefinger by his bedside.

So long to the palm of your mother on your sweating forehead
while you were throwing up in the toilet.

So long to the measured ascent of your hand along the widening thigh
of Jane who could have easily slapped you.

It was just the opposite.
Whatever it was – and it was multitudinous –

I could not love it enough.
What my consciousness was
was the consciousness of others. Past and Present.

You'll see what I mean a thousand years from now.

The Swan's Song

From what I understand a swan
conveys her innermost feelings with a hiss or a snort.

That seems to me like a joke.
For example, have you ever heard a swan snort?

Otherwise the swan, except for the agitated clapping of wings,
is serene as a sharecropper being shaved in a small town in Alabama in 1953.

Delilah communicates her love for her eternal mate in ways
unbeknownst to us –
like how a wife of a long time might close her eyes

scrubbing that night's dishes when her husband begins to massage
her neck from behind with his forefinger and thumb.

His eyes closed as well. So a swan's song must refer to the quiet
that arrives at the conclusion
to talking and writing down an elegy hurriedly for oneself, right?

Side by side, never far apart. Sampson in love. Delilah in love.
The gentlest of ripples
widening with mathematical precision

behind them on green scum. Scooping their beaks intermittently
so as to suppress what they really would like to say.
Silence so much more rewarding.
One then the other following the other for life.

You were so close

You were on that threshold
of knowing it all,
while at the same time having your heart in the right place.

So far away it is now.
Vivid as never before.

You were more than a little justified
in being upset
seeing one chick's head after the other twisted

then cast aside like dice in a casino

by your nephew Andrew whom you were always afraid of.
Their little yellow torsos ran round and round
in a panic to understand why.

*

I love that wide-eyed child
shimmying up one of our three cottonwoods in his pajamas
so he could see
in a far more personal light than the one that illuminated
supernovas in his science class
a deity full of dawns and full of evenings.

My mother, after her husband died with his eyes off to the side
before her eyes
listened to Lawerence Welk every Sunday night

and reveled in black and white photographs
of the past.

You were stupid.
You behaved like a horse's ass.
And you were loved.

Four

You should never use the word beautiful

the bitter poet told me
from across the laminated table in Tuscaloosa over a Heineken.
Now, when I think back on what he spat out, his eyes flashing

back and forth at the loud clientele – hunter or hunted
I knew not – I still can't comprehend why
he might have said that to me. It's been years.
The trees, as they were for Yeats

when he counted out those fifty-nine swans,
were in their autumn beauty that Friday night
outside Lee's Tomb, the bluegrass band tuning up.
Even then, as I listened, I dared not disagree

with the assertions of one
who spoke viciously of everyone who crossed him.
I have thought of him, since we parted,
not often. I think of him now,

having come across one of Keats' letters at the end of his life
"I have loved the principle of beauty in everything"
and wish I had known that sentence before he got up –
one among several irrefutable voices

I could have flung up at him before he swayed off
taking his and all other doctrines with him into the night.

Blue Estuaries

Please don't forget Bogan, to you out there.
Louise was all in from the very beginning

 and never got over what it means to be appalled.
Or else let Bogan go with all of her
clear words: "clean wood cleft by an ax."

Finding your way to her as a writer takes a long time.
After her brief emphatic reading in California

my friend and mentor approached her with her Blue Estuaries

and wondered why
she would say that she did not write anymore

to which this dignified marvel shot back
"Because it is too hard."

Bogan, alone, in her modest apartment in New York
with the bedsheets thrashed about.

She meant a lot to me and when someone means a lot to you
you want others to care as well.

I would like to be kinder

to Kevin above all
lip-syncing behind the counter at the supermarket at Whitaker Square
to the muted overhead music,

adjusting my most mundane groceries in the paper bag
he shakes open with a snap
after saying my first name. I have meandered here for years

up and down the fluorescent aisles
of meat and potatoes with Barry Manilow singing Copacabana.

It's hard not to get infuriated
in this world that seems unable to find its ass with its own hands.

Let it go,
And don't be sentimental.

God is not love.
Nor is beauty.

Truth covers it all.
So says Mister Wiseman who has lately turned seventy

in a universe that scared the bejusus out of Blaise Pascal
and that could turn out to be as trivial

as an itsy bitsy pinprick for all we know,
revolving around Kevin and Blaise and all the rest of us
as we revolve around everyone we love.

Silent

mysterious Cynthia,
one hand tucked inside the lining of her cardigan jacket…
she's watching with such concentration
her pint-sized dog Lollie
chase and be chased around by my dog at the park.

Cynthia's whole immediate life:

eleventh-floor apartment, her unwed hand held out to Lollie.
Fingers fluttering. Come my love.
Floc on the walls, potpourri by the door bolted shut,

one bedroom out of two painted cherry-blossom pink with a fold-out
couch no one knows about
except an ecstatic Pekingese with a streak of milk on her upper lip
that can't get enough of her and vice versa.

This is a matter of enormous importance to me this morning
and tells me almost all that I need to know
about being alive among others.

I let the handyman in

to fix the wounded pipe that drools
and he says "Ah," seeing my book on North American birds
on the table,
"I used to have one just like that,"
then spreads his tools out on the linoleum
and stares up under the sink,
jiggling that upper intestine of metal
with forefinger and thumb.
And he speaks of his divorce.

Miles is playing on the stereo later
when I hear whistling,
nothing to parallel the rhythm
of that trumpet turning around, receding,
curving back. How does Davis do us like that?
What's underneath the sink begins to relent
and I'm standing over him
asking, "Do you make emergency house calls?"
He doesn't answer,
although there is this noticeable loosening in the muscles
in his neck when he says,
"To this day I don't know why she left me."

This Ancient Study

After Phil had stepped out for his daily workout
I wandered into his study at the back of their house.

There was so much going on in my head
that I could hardly see what was there.

This is where, for so much of his life, Phil Levine sat
in that leather chair with his legs crossed, his thin right leg

draped over the other casually, one of his many fountain pens
that he collected poised above the yellow lined paper

on which he wrote me letters for three decades.
How could he do so without smoking a cigarette?

And all those worn volumes behind him and to his right
in alphabetical order, above all that tan chapbook

by his former student Ernesto Trejo,
to whom he wrote one of his most beautiful elegies,

most, I imagine, sent to this truth-teller, myself included,
by those who wanted his applause.

I'm thinking now of his kind wife Franny firing off a glance
with her cat Miranda in her arms into the dark room of his study

in their one-story house I remember for its orange trees.
I believe she sees him there as I do.

I've come to love the freckled middle-aged face of Lori

at the pharmacy drive in window. She is so enamored of my dog Buddie.
I roll down the rear window so she can
slip him a biscuit, reaching back, for I have moved

my Toyota a little bit forward. I, having dematerialized
in her adoration of those brown uplifted compliant eyes,

hear her say to Buddie what would be nice for Lori to say to me.
You sweetheart. You beautiful boy.

Lori hands me my antidepressant, Wellbutrin,
all the while drawn to my dog's countenance.

No shame in that. I told Jessica once you have to be
really fucked up not to be on antidepressants

in this day and age. If Christ were on Prozac,
would he have not said he was the Way

and the Truth and the Life? Lori's eyes light up.
She's smiling so kindly down and over my shoulder
at the auburn eyes of one who is as close to providence

as is possible. "Have a great day!"
All days are great though, Lori, when the days are numbered now.

Peace to marry purpose – purpose to marry grace.
That's the way I see things now in my eighth decade.

And there where the garden path on November mornings

is the loneliest, on the slope,
an old Chilean prestidigitator mopes, hunched over.
He is contemplating a spotted blossom that seems so inconsequential
it steers him back to his own death in the cold.

Neruda. Pondering row on row of desiccated chrysanthemums and
roses. In his frayed overcoat. I would like to approach him,
tap his shoulder, say *gracias* for his time on earth. It is enough to know,
his songs drawing to a close, that I saw him once in passing
in my dream of a winter garden years ago.

Five

That Disconcerting Epiphany

Everything seems just fine and dandy to me this
evening
until the death of someone
who turned gently away
in bed after making love
body to body
that is far more stunning now than it was
even at the moment of orgasm
in 1999

gets up out of the afterlife
with all of her accusations behind her
and announces
"all of it was not folly
but a helluva lot of it was"

folly
in retrospect
what tanned Ulysses
must have felt if he was honest with himself
when Penelope
opened her white, slender, aged arms to him
even though he had disguised himself

because
after all
was he not just a child?

That arrow aimed at the heart
that caress
that will never be a caress again
death and sex
as ordinary as sitting down for supper
as extraordinary as getting up in the morning
to look at the clock.

I had to laugh

when Louie quoted Christ after Christ was crucified.
Approached by Magdalene who wanted to touch one more time

the rejuvenated Messiah after realizing that he had not left them
all behind.
Noli me tangere – *Don't touch me, I'm divine.*

If you think you know silence
ask one of the dead to speak up and you will be shocked

by how silence is redefined.
It's comical when a friend of forty years draws back,

smiling: *Don't touch me, I'm divine.*
Christ in that cave. A vapor. Poof. And he is gone.

I touched my mother's wide creased brow cautiously
just after she entered the afterlife
and she never said anything remotely like Noli me tangere.

Don't you think Jesus should have just let Magdalene wrap
her aromatic arms around his bony shoulders,

pardoned later for surrendering
to another one's craving to be even closer than before?

Who wouldn't want to understand

if only a little
the crimson choreography of those cardinals, why

 one rockets off when another cardinal panics below the porch.
And what the easy going rapport is between male
and female,
the former much more spectacularly colorful this spring.

That dance, that competition. The coyness before coming close,
that territorial insistence. Then the formidable aria
in dawnlight
you just wish would shut the hell up.

 Wishes.
You could follow all of them back to adolescence
then see what you wished for never came to pass.

Maybe one of them,
that's about it.
The wish to be you at this moment in your life came true
and that in itself is miraculous.

Neither Tony nor Jane nor Lucia can see

what I see, my ankles crossed on this stone bench
under an always ephemeral afternoon sun in whatever month.

I had no idea the flow of the widest clouds
represented so well the solemn passage of eternity.

Not only days, not only months,
seasons, centuries, millennia.

What a fool I would be not to give thought
to what the recently deceased are deprived of witnessing.

Tony realized this in that last year of pancreatic cancer
and Jane never saw such things in the first place.

Pain had turned her away.
The generations, one just as indispensable as the next one.

Tony marveled, having set his magnificent rage aside.
And Jane listened to Bach's Cello Suites in the end with Kathleen.

Look at that crawling cloud with an outline of amber.
It will soon be yours to see.

For now, I follow it
from one end of the firmament to the other.

Even Lucia in the end wrote beautifully of a curtain
in the breeze. And I can hardly believe what I am seeing.

In The Cool Heart Of Morning

In the cool heart of morning
I find Black-eyed Susans on the hill
      and bring them down to the house
   to lay them on the table.

      Where is the crystal vase
    that could contain this scattered elegance

of petals wet and shining?

 Their shape must be just right,
       so that a couple dining
    won't be distracted. Fretting over the arrangement

     of the stems,
  my fingers separate the ones

that cling, as if they were afraid of me, leaves overlapping leaves,
  one sibling struggling to get above the rest.

   And I
  who have lavished such attention
       on the strongest blossom
  with a grave downward look

   sigh,
resigning myself to what can't satisfy the eye.

Sitting down to supper though
I contemplate this perfection on the table,

a bouquet of Black-eyed Susans freshly picked,
misshapen, in disarray.

And fall in love with everything again.

(spring 1983)

This is my life, not yours

This is my life, not yours.
Yours, mine. Mine, yours. Yours.

Whitman began his long *Song Of Myself*
with the word "I" and concluded with the word
"you."

Meaning you.
Meaning me.

Six

Galilee

Oh, I'm all right,
slinking a little self consciously into and out of the lives of others.

What would it be like, though, to roll over while yawning
to another breathing body on Easter morning?

Saints and angels. Assholes – an honorable man scrambling
out of bed after underlining a passage from Leviticus

in one of the suburbs in Seattle to cradle that newborn
that even now in the night light looks so much like her mother.

I missed the boat.
But don't you know, there was another boat of sorts
that summoned me to hang on tight.

Which I did prior to climbing the mast
with increasing confidence to see what might be out there.

Last Leaf

I've been waiting on and off
so I could bear witness in my misanthropic oddity
to that orange leaf giving in
to the winter gusts predicted by the weatherman last evening.

From the very beginning I had a pretty good idea
this was a reluctant leaf.
Its kinsmen could no longer look it in the face.
They had already undertaken the final journey.

Rollicking back and forth. Twirling. It was both an elegiac
and joyous occasion.
That last leaf clung to the otherwise abandoned branch.

Then for whatever reason it was set free from my cherry tree
the morning before the first snow of the year
making it clear after such single mindedness

it was more than a little proud of its achievement.
It flipped one underside up to me

then that other side to me in the light of the sun
as an illustration of how I too should behave.

Should I have lingered longer

over what it means to see the sun's light giving in
to the afterthought of evening shadows?

It came to me again today on my porch of limitless possibilities,
that inquisitive flicker
made famous by Johannes Vermeer on the wall in that painting
from which he has exquisitely disappeared.

A conceited crow strides there in that shadow
and has no idea that it is being observed.

Up and away.
Then the merest stirring of wind in the holly
making those shadows shiver.

Night in the fields. And the new moon there.

And the moon belonging to the moon. Night and the many stars.
What the beloved brings to the turning earth in June

and the turning earth to the beloved. Sanctity of crickets.
And the famished and silent in sunlight Christ

understanding if only for a moment or so
all of the stars. Ethereal figure. I listen

within the myth this side of the singing needlegrass.
More than a grave – a conversation with the deceased.

Dialogue of wind. And what it means to be human.
Night and the dip and sway and flow, a long stream

of shimmering sycamores along the Missouri River
that curves away. Night in the fields and the moon ascending.

What More Might There Be For You To Say?

Just shut up.
You have said everything possible about that flash in the pan
called your life.

It was a fine thing to be alive.
Even when your up-and-coming wife with dollar signs
on her mind paced robotically in her chemise

between the tiny dining room table and the chifferobe
in the claustrophobic house you shared on Lake Forest Drive,
toiling to come
to some conclusion over the course of an hour

if she should put her foot down
or let bygones be bygones. It could have gone either way.
Hilarious, to think about that now.
You slapped your troubled stepson Douglas on the head

caught lighting a ferocious flame
using an aerosol in the sun room some thirty years ago.

Okay. There are a multitude of such moments
you would be wise to probably keep your mouth
shut about. But you are not wise. So carry on.

Let that moth fighting for her life

about the size of a snowflake whirl
then risk an odyssey that doesn't last long
into the darkness of this summer.

Nope. Comes back,
circles the little light on my porch,

buoyant: the vanilla candle my sister bought for me
at The Dollar Store
after the surgery on my ankle that put me in a wheelchair
for three months, that is so intriguing.

How dare you sweep your hand before this inveterate seeker
when you could as easily
let her go on living for another day?

So small, I can't see the fluttering of her wings.
Of so little importance you should go back to dreaming

and giving the middle finger

up at that hotshot cutting in front of you
in his cherry-red Camaro, its top down, on Reynolda Road.

But eight decades on this planet say, if they had the tongue,
"Follow that flutter with your forefinger up into the light."

Then let it go whatever way it wishes into the night
you, too, are more than a little frightened of.

Old Age

Light.
Then darkness that historically is fond of what will take
its place in the sky.

I'm not scared by the changing of the guard.
Shadows darken.

Light zeroing in on those numberless gnats ecstatic to exist
on the brighter side of the only blue spruce in the yard.
They rise and they fall.

Dark, my light,
darker, my desire.

That flirtatious yellow ray
that shudders delicately to rest on my mantelpiece.

And I am looking over my shoulder
through my front window to see from where it might be issuing.

I like the darkness,
as long as I am not in pain,

which is why I have always loved
what is called Night-Blooming Cereus.

The darkness says "Come here.
I will take care of you."

And the light: "You're able to do this,
if you just get out of your bed."

He had hoped

to get up that horrible morning after going through withdrawals to a lumber
colored doe and a fawn making every effort to keep up

 as if in a drifting dream of another drifting life.

Lacking that – an elephant, perhaps, with her stumbling newborn under her,
plopping dung while yanking leaves of the maple down

beside his dilapidated fence

would be nice.
What he woke up to though was the Lord's Prayer on his lips,

scant sunlight splintering through high cumulus clouds.
Everything in the reddish brown of autumn. Amen.

What he wanted – what he would settle for.

The doe, with that uncertain insouciant white-spotted fawn,
the elephant, her trunk swaying under her paunch
to feel for once more
what she had given birth to on the savannah the previous morning.

He gave a lot of thought to this.
Then gave too his vision two arthritic thumbs up:

a water buffalo in Kenya eye to eye with him –
that spectacular black eye of one who hates you
even though he has no idea who you are.

What must it be like for you, you

less than a mosquito – minuscule – up there

obsessively stroking your silvery translucent wings
on the light of my table lamp

above my squinting eyes in the otherwise darkness?
What could possibly be more fragile than you?

Then you pace round and round
this circular perimeter of light that's supposed to shine eternally –

a rebellious William Blake with ink all over his fingers and cheeks
who out of frustration and in a metaphysical rush

finally said to old Nobadaddy,
"Go into a circle and see how you would do."

Humans.
They are so huge compared to you.

Even my finger is humongous.
And I see the illuminated left front leg hesitate

before electing to dismiss the seductive forefinger
stretched out in Michelangelo's Sistine Chapel ceiling.

No way.
You are too busy living for just one day.

John Clare

What seemed so small to Clare at first
seemed all the world.

Pakistan, Mogadishu, El Paso, Northampton.
The procession of wolves across
the new-fallen snow somewhere below the pole,

with an elk with its nostrils held high trying to rejoin the herd.
What was private became, over time, the way of all flesh.

The big intimidating Charles Mingus in Cuernavaca
in his jet black suit
stopping his fingers tapping across the strings of his bass

after hearing someone laugh out loud in the dark, saying:
"Isaac Stern didn't have to put up with this shit."

And Clare saw the configuration of a gray squirrel
manipulating its four fingers, much like a fly,

one of the seeds he had side-armed out. It was all there
for him after months of waiting for the chipmunk with one ear

he referred to as Minnie
to stuff that unsalted peanut on the porch into her mouth.

Not even his catheter kept him from loving what he saw.
You know who he is. He knows too.

He and I and you and her pulling a wooden cart
of one's belongings
on the interminable dirt road leading

out of Paris

and Mister You-Know-Who slapping a mosquito
that was Jewish
on his wrist, then looking down derisively to see

if there might be

a splat of Aryan blood there on his palm
drawn from the capillaries of the devil on mescaline.

For Over Fifty Years

For over fifty years
these words have thirsted. Taking up my long life
in their hands they tipped back the chalice, drank
my father's death, drank my mother's silence.

I would like to learn how to care for
my life that gave such sustenance to these utterances.
I see it now, as one coming into a theater.
I step carefully up the narrow unlit aisle.

Everyone there looks away from me in that sacramental darkness.
Some whisper. Some seem touched.
They laugh as I take my seat near the back.
This is my life. It is not a caricature. You can't just laugh

because it turned out cockeyed or wrong,
because you yourself think you have it all figured out.
There. That's better. Now eat your buttered popcorn
and watch what is given to all of us,

this life you can't under any circumstances take back,
that blew past you, remembered in flickering instants
with all of its horrors, all of its doubts,
that you have begun so late to love as though it were yours.

Can I Give You This

Can I hold this out to you
and know that you will
appreciate what I have
ministered to, polished, honed, shaped,
spit-shined, sanded, polished,
put away and dreamed of
and changed and became dissatisfied with,
adored, coveted, placed in the blazing sun
in a fit of frustration
over how imperfect it now is?

Here, I am sick of it,
can't live without it, never want to see it again,
can't take my eyes away
even as I hold this out to you this morning,
this afternoon, this night,
this nothingness that began as something
then suffered to the point
where it had no choice but to become
what I craved, hoping you would crave it too,
a husk, first turned to dust,
then to the very air you breathe,
an icon that does not exist.

Will you take this? And then cherish
what is invisible and limitless
in its capacity to sustain you?
Here. You can have it. It is yours.

The End

www.ingramcontent.com/pod-product-compliance
Lightning Source LLC
Chambersburg PA
CBHW060537080526
44586CB00012B/775